Earth in Space

by Donna Latham

PEARSON
Scott
Foresman

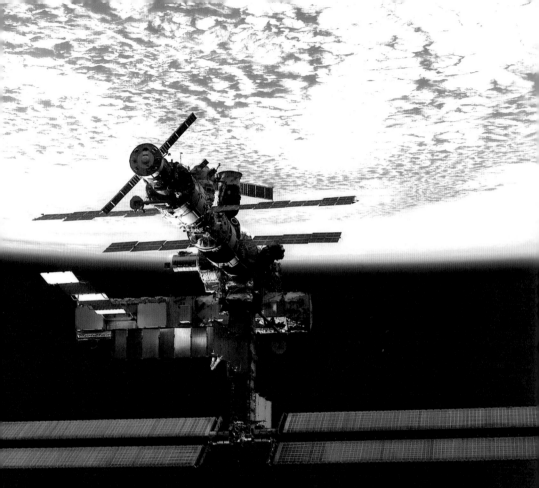

In what ways does Earth move?

Earth's Orbit

Earth is a small, blue, ball-shaped planet. It has one moon. Along with eight other planets and the Sun, it is one of the main parts of the **solar system.** Each of the planets follows its own path around the Sun. This path is called an orbit. Orbit paths are not exactly round. They are elliptical, or shaped like

A **revolution** is one orbit. It takes Earth just a little more than 365 days to make its revolution around the Sun. Does 365 sound like a familiar number to you? It should! It's a year. The Moon's revolution around Earth doesn't take nearly that long. It takes only twenty-eight days, or about a month.

What causes planets to orbit the Sun? It's the gravity between the Sun and the planets. Gravity is the force that pulls things down toward Earth's surface. It keeps them from zooming out into space. The pull of the Sun's gravity is very strong. It causes the planets to move in elliptical paths, rather than in straight lines.

Day and Night

As you read this, what time of day is it? When our part of Earth faces the Sun, we have day. When it turns away from the Sun, we have night. The constant spinning of Earth causes the changes of day and night.

If you have ever spun a top, you know that it tilts, or leans as it moves. A top spins around an imaginary line called an **axis.** Earth spins, or rotates, on an axis too.

This diagram shows Earth's tilt. It also shows its spin. The North Pole is at the top of the axis. The South Pole is at the bottom.

Earth's axis is an imaginary line. It is not really there. But if you picture it in your mind, you can see how Earth spins.

A **rotation** is one spin of an object on its axis. Earth completes a rotation in twenty-four hours. That's one day. Earth's tilt causes some parts of the planet to receive more daylight than others. Depending on where people live, the length of day and night changes all year. The change is more noticeable in some places than others. On one day in spring and one day in fall, day and night are the same length.

Earth's Comfortable Temperature

And what's the temperature today where you live? Thanks to the speed of Earth's rotation, day follows night quickly. So, the Earth does not get too hot or too cold. Earth also has an atmosphere, or layer of gases, to help control temperature. It reflects some of the Sun's rays to keep us cool, but also traps some to keep us warm.

The Pattern of Seasons

The pattern of changes which we call the seasons is caused by Earth's tilt. Earth always tilts the same way during its orbit. So at different times of year, different parts of Earth tilt toward the Sun. Those parts receive more daylight hours. They are also warmer, because sunlight hits them at a more direct angle. Daylight lasts longer in the summer. It is shorter in the winter.

Look at the diagram. It shows Earth's revolution around the Sun. Do you see how the Sun is off to the side of Earth's orbit? It is not exactly in the middle. The distance between Earth and the Sun changes throughout the year. But this distance does not affect our seasons.

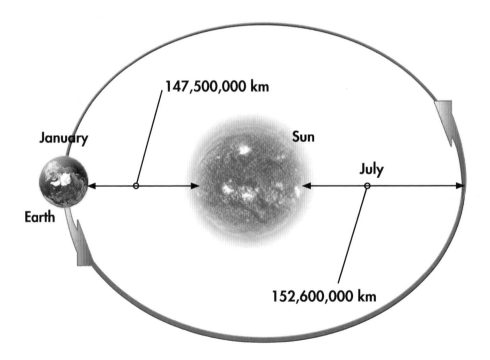

Earth's Seasons

This diagram shows the seasons for the Northern Hemisphere, where the United States is located. The seasons change as the Earth orbits the Sun. But the tilt of Earth's axis never changes.

Around June 21: Summer The North Pole tilts toward the Sun. The Sun's most direct rays fall on the Northern Hemisphere. So it has the most daylight hours and becomes warmer.

Around March 21: Spring The North Pole starts to slant toward the Sun. Now the hours of daylight and night are equal.

You are here

Around September 21: Fall begins in the Northern Hemisphere. The hours of daylight and night are equal.

Around December 21: Winter The North Pole has its greatest slant away from the Sun. Daylight is shorter than on any other day of the year.

What are the parts of the solar system?

Venus

Mars

Mercury

Earth

Jupiter

Saturn

asteroid belt

Our solar system is made up of the Sun and its nine planets. This diagram shows the position of the planets in the solar system. The diagram is not to scale, because if it were, it would not fit on the page. The planets are too far apart. You don't even need a telescope to see many of the planets in the sky. Planets close to the Sun move quickly and have small orbits. Planets far from the Sun move slowly and have large orbits. Their revolutions take many Earth years.

Because the planets are so far away from one another, and space is so huge, the units of measure we use on Earth don't work very well. They are much too small. Scientists use AUs, or astronomical units, instead of miles or kilometers. One AU equals about 150 million kilometers.

Uranus

Neptune

Pluto

Planet	Distance from the Sun	Temperatures
Mercury	4.0 AU	-290 to +800°F (-170 to +430°C)
Venus	.7 AU	+860°F (+460°C)
Earth	1.0 AU	-130 to +140°F (-90 to +60°C)
Mars	1.5 AU	-220 to +60°F (-140 to +20°C)
Jupiter	5.2 AU	-220°F (-140°C)
Saturn	9.5 AU	-290°F (-180°C)
Uranus	19.2 AU	-360°F (-220°C)
Neptune	30.0 AU	-350°F (-210°C)
Pluto	39.5 AU	-390 to -370°F (-230 to -220°C)

Visiting the Planets

Space probes have been used to explore the planets for years. **Space probes** are spacecraft that can gather data without any people aboard to run them. But they do carry special instruments. With them, space probes find out about planet surfaces and what they are made of.

Mariner 10, a space probe, flew by Mercury and Venus in the 1970s.

In 2004, the Mars rovers *Spirit* and *Opportunity* were landed on Mars. They sent color pictures back to Earth.

Mercury

Scientists think Mercury's core is mostly made of iron. Mercury's surface temperature can go from -170°C to 970°C .

Venus

Venus is the closest planet to Earth. Venus is just as hot during the night as it is during the day. That's because the Sun's heat gets trapped in the planet's thick clouds. Venus's atmosphere is made up of poisonous gases.

Mars

Mars has giant volcanoes. It looks red because of the reddish-brown iron in its soil. Mars also has ice caps at its poles.

The Gas Giants

Past Mars are four "gas giant" planets. They are Jupiter, Saturn, Uranus, and Neptune. These huge planets are gigantic balls of gas. We have discovered moons and rings around all the gas giants.

Pluto

Scientists think Pluto is made of ice and rock. It has a moon, which is about the same size as the planet itself!

What are comets and asteroids?

Comets

Comets are icy, dusty masses orbiting the Sun. There may also be rocky matter inside them. Much smaller than planets, comets come from beyond Pluto. Their paths are very stretched out.

Each year, a few comets enter our solar system and circle the Sun. But only the very largest ones can be seen without a telescope.

nucleus

A comet's nucleus has an uneven shape. Scientists call it a "dirty snowball." Made of dust and ice, the nucleus grows black and solid over time. The nucleus is very small, sometimes only a few kilometers across.

A comet is made up of a solid core called a nucleus and a cloud of dust and gas called a coma. Look at the diagram to learn more about each part of a comet.

two tails

Comets have two tails. They stream out in a direction away from the Sun. The tails may be up to 80 million kilometers long! The ion tail is made of tiny, magnetic particles of gas. It is thin and blue in color and sticks straight out from the comet. The dust tail is wide and yellow. It is made of dust that is released by the melting nucleus.

coma

Around the nucleus is a giant cloud of dust and gases. The coma can be even larger than the planet Jupiter. The fine dust reflects sunlight brightly. The gases take in energy and glow. It's the coma that gives a comet its fuzzy look. The coma and tail form only when the comet gets close to the Sun. There, sunlight melts part of the nucleus.

Asteroids

An **asteroid** is a rocky mass that revolves around the Sun and is much smaller than a planet. Asteroids can be several hundred kilometers wide, but some are as tiny as pebbles. Many asteroids have odd, uneven shapes. And some even have smaller asteroids that orbit them. Jupiter's gravity holds most asteroids in a belt beyond Mars, but occasionally one will hit Earth. Take a look at these images of asteroids.

by a nose
Here's an asteroid with an odd shape! Some people think it looks like a flying nose. The largest asteroids, though, are more ball-shaped, like the planets.

asteroid Eros
Look at the surface of Eros. Can you spot the craters, boulders, and rock layers? More than thirty three kilometers long and thirteen kilometers thick, Eros is the first asteroid to be landed on by a spacecraft.

asteroid Ida
Ida is about fifty eight kilometers long and twenty three wide. It is in the asteroid belt between Mars and Jupiter.

Meteors, Meteoroids, and Meteorites

Small asteroids called meteoroids are usually the size of a grain of sand but can be as big as a boulder. When they hit Earth's atmosphere, they become meteors. They heat up and make a glowing streak across the night sky. You may have seen this happen but called it by a different name: a shooting star. Very bright shooting stars are called fireballs. When Earth passes through the cloud of matter left behind by a comet, we see many meteors at once. This is called a meteor shower.

Arizona's Meteor Crater

Although most meteors burn up before they crash into Earth, some do not. Then, pieces of them may fall to Earth. A meteorite is a piece of rock or metal that has fallen from space. Most are very small, but sometimes a large one lands, causing great damage.

This crater was caused by a small meteorite. It is about two hundred meters deep and twelve hundred meters across.

What is Known about the Moon?

Traveling with Earth

At about 384,000 kilometers (238,000 miles) away, the Moon is Earth's closest neighbor in the solar system. You might not think that sounds very close. But compared to everything else in our solar system, the Moon is right next door!

The Moon is the only place, other than Earth, where people have stood. It is also Earth's only natural satellite. A **satellite** is an object in orbit around another object.

This crater was caused by an object crashing into the moon.

The Moon's Surface

The Moon is covered with mountains, craters, and smooth plains. You can see them in this photo. The Moon has no air or water, although it does have some ice. At one time lava flowed on the Moon, creating large areas of smooth rock.

Visiting the Moon

On July 20, 1969, Neil Armstrong became the first person to step on the Moon. From 1969 to 1972, twelve people walked on the Moon.

Looking at the Moon

As the Moon orbits Earth, we can see only one side. Called the near side, this half of the Moon faces Earth at all times. That's because the moon spins and orbits at about the same speed.

This is the near side of the Moon. That's the half that faces Earth, and the side we see.

Neil Armstrong

A satellite took this photo of the far side of the Moon.

Phases of the Moon

Have you noticed that the Moon appears to change shape at different times of the month? These different shapes are called **Moon phases.**

Although the Moon often looks very bright in the sky, it doesn't really produce any light. "Moonlight" is really sunlight reflecting off the Moon's surface. Only one side of the Moon is lit by the Sun. At different times of the month, different amounts of the lit side face Earth. This is why the Moon seems to change shape.

When we see the Moon from Earth, we see its lit side. As the Moon orbits Earth, different amounts of this side can be seen.

Over a month, the Moon appears in different shapes. We call them phases.

Sunday	Monday	Tuesday	Wednesday	Thursday	Friday	Saturday
					1	2
3	4	5	6	7	8	9
10	11	12	13	14	15	16
17	18	19	20	21	22	23
24	25	26	27	28	29	30

View from Earth

New Moon
You can hardly see a new Moon! It passes between the Earth and the Sun. The side in shadow faces Earth. The sunlit side faces away.

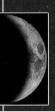

Crescent Moon
For a few days after the new Moon, you can see a crescent Moon. It is a little slice of the Moon's sunlit side.

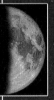

First quarter Moon
The first quarter Moon is seen about a week after the new Moon. Half of the Moon's sunlit side faces Earth.

Full Moon
You can see the full Moon about a week after the first quarter. Earth is between the Moon and the Sun.

High and Low Tides

If you've ever spent a day at the beach, you know that the ocean has high and low tides. The water level rises for six hours and then goes back down for another six hours. There are two high tides and two low tides each day.

The Moon's gravity causes the tides. It makes the ocean bulge out toward the Moon. Tides are high in the areas that bulge out, and low in the areas that don't. As the Moon moves around Earth, the bulge moves with it, causing the high tides to travel around the world.

The Bay of Fundy is famous for its tides. They are the highest in the world, reaching fifteen meters (fifty feet). At low tide, boats end up sitting in the mud!

The Sun's gravity affects the tides too. But it is a much smaller effect than the Moon's. During a new Moon, the Sun, Earth, and Moon are all lined up. At this time the highest tides take place. At the first quarter or third quarter moon, things are different! The Sun pulls on Earth at one angle. The Moon pulls at another. This causes the lowest tides, or the neap tides.

In this short journey around the solar system, you've learned many things. You have learned that it is made up of the Sun and its satellites—including Earth. You have also learned that the Moon, meteors, comets, and asteroids are also part of the solar system.

You have learned that Earth's orbit causes many things to happen. For example, day becomes night. Seasons change. Tides rise and fall. And the phases of the Moon occur each month. Our neighbors in the solar system may be far away, but they have a big effect on our world!

Glossary

asteroid   a rocky mass orbiting the Sun that is less than a thousand kilometers across.

axis   the imaginary line around which a planet rotates, or spins.

comet   a frozen mass of ice, rock, and dust that orbits the Sun and forms bright clouds and long tails.

Moon phase   the shape changes the Moon goes through in a month.

revolution   one trip of a planet or another object around its orbit.

rotation   one whole spin of an object around its axis.

satellite   an object that orbits another.

solar system   the Sun and its satellites.

space probe   a spacecraft that gathers data without a crew.